Everyday Vocabulary Builders

Write Better. Write Faster.

Ashan R. Hampton

Cornerstone Publishing
Arkansas

Published by Cornerstone Communications & Publishing, Little Rock, Arkansas.

Cover Design: Ashan R. Hampton
Cover Photo: © *Can Stock Photo/grgroup*

Websites: www.arhampton.com
www.prowritingskills.com

Library of Congress Control Number: 2019911800
ISBN: 978-0-359-84868-3

Printed in the United States of America.

First Edition.

Cataloging-in-Publication Data is on file with the Library of Congress.

10 9 8 7 6 5 4 3 2 1

Student Success

Online Classes

Graduate Research Writing

Student Success Essay Writing

Student Success Grammar Skills

Student Success Writing Skills

www.arhampton.com
www.prowritingskills.com

About the Author

Ashan R. Hampton has worked as an English instructor in higher education for over 20 years, most notably at Morehouse College in Atlanta, Georgia. She is also a proud graduate of the *Donaghey Scholars Program* at the University of Arkansas at Little Rock under the direction of Dr. C. Earl Ramsey, Emeritus.

Ashan's original research, *History of the Arkansas State Hospital 1859-1930*, was published in the *Pulaski County Historical Review* (1995), and continues to be cited by history scholars today. Her articles on notable African American Arkansans also appear in the *Encyclopedia of Arkansas History and Culture*.

With her doctoral studies on hold, Ashan has found success in online education. She produces and teaches her own writing and grammar courses for global audiences through her company, Cornerstone Communications & Publishing. Ashan is also a published author, digital media producer, proofreader and copyeditor.

Visit her website: **www.arhampton.com**.

More Books by Ashan R. Hampton

Grammar Essentials for Proofreading, Copyediting &
Business Writing
ISBN: 978-1-387-91413-5

Student Success Grammar Skills
ISBN: 978-0-359-60763-1

Proofreading Power: Skills & Drills
ISBN: 978-1-387-95472-8

Adult Learner Grammar Essentials
ISBN: 978-0-359-69282-8

Urban Grammar Quick Fixes (B & W)
ISBN: 978-1-329-91923-5

Start Your Proofreading Side-Hustle: Maximize
Your Writing Skills
ISBN: 978-1-077-54526-7

Start Your Proofreading Business: Maximize
Your Writing Skills
ISBN: 978-1-079-13488-9

Contents

"Words, once they're printed,
have a life of their own."
--CAROL BURNETT

abundant *adj.* (*uh*-**buhn**-d*uh*nt): a large amount: more than enough.

 📖 Community groups bought an ***abundant*** supply of snacks for the afterschool tutoring program.

belligerent *adj.* (b*uh*-**lij**-er-*uh*nt): having an aggressive or fighting attitude; to be hostile or combative.

 📖 Tammy became ***belligerent*** when the server messed up her order.

caboose *n.* (k*uh*-**boos**): the last car at the back of a train; someone or something that brings up the rear; buttocks.

 📖 The tuba player is the ***caboose*** of the marching band's line formation.

deceive *v.* (dee-**seev**): to trick or lead astray by cheating, being dishonest or creating a false impression.

 📖 Credit card companies ***deceive*** college students with hidden fees, late charges and high interest rates.

eager *adj.* (**ee**-ger): impatient enthusiasm or desire; ready to make something happen.

 📖 The kids were ***eager*** to take a field trip to the Mid-America science museum with their teacher.

famished *adj.* (**fam**-isht): intensely hungry.

 📖 After three hours of practice, the football players were ***famished***.

genuine *adj.* (**jen**-yoo-in): actual; true; produced by or proceeding from the original source; heart-felt, sincere or honest expressions of feelings.

📖 Rodney proposed to Erica with a ***genuine***, 3-carat pink diamond.

habitable *adj.* (**hab**-i-t*uh*-b*uh* l): capable of being lived in; suitable to use as living quarters or housing.

📖 Camping tents for the homeless are not ideal, but ***habitable***.

ideal *n.* (ahy-**dee**-*uh*l): a standard or model of perfection, beauty or excellence; a goal; a favorable or preferred condition.

📖 Karen went on a diet to reach her ***ideal*** dress size before the wedding.

jovial *adj.* (**joe**-vee-*uh*l): having a good attitude; full of joy; friendly, fun or sociable.

📖 At school, Jeremy joined a group of ***jovial,*** creative art students.

Vocabulary Exercise #1

Directions: Choose the correct definition.

1. abundant

    a) scarce
    b) overflowing
    c) rich

2. jovial

    a) mean and sad
    b) fun and joyful
    c) antisocial

3. ideal

    a) a high standard
    b) unpleasant goal
    c) low quality

4. belligerent

    a) loving
    b) kind
    c) hostile

5. famished

    a) impatient
    b) hungry
    c) satisfied

6. habitable

    a) condemned
    b) moveable
    c) livable

7. caboose

    a) the back
    b) the front
    c) the side

8. genuine

    a) false
    b) inferior
    c) true

9. deceive

    a) to care
    b) to trick
    c) to talk

10. eager

    a) unavailable
    b) patient
    c) ready

Answers on the back of this page.

Answers: Vocabulary Exercise #1

1. b

2. b

3. a

4. c

5. b

6. c

7. a

8. c

9. b

10. c

Your Score

_____ correct out of 10

10 – 100%
9 – 90%
8 – 80%
7 – 70%
6 – 60%
5 – 50%
4 – 40%
3 – 30%
2 – 20%
1 – 10%

100%........Excellent
90-80%......Good
70%..........Fair
60%..........Keep Practicing

A score chart does not follow every exercise, on purpose. Some people like them, but some do not. We have tried to accommodate both.

"If it takes a lot of words to say what you have in mind, give it more thought."
-- DENNIS ROTH

kinetic *adj.* (ki-**net**-ik): related to motion; active; lively; dynamic.

📖 The *kinetic* energy of the dance team made the audience stand and shout.

latitude *n.* (**lat**-i-tood): the distance north or south from the earth's equator measured by angles and degrees; freedom from restrictions; the freedom to take action and make choices.

📖 My parents give me the *latitude* to have fun without a curfew.

maintain *v.* (mane-**tane**): to preserve from failure or decline; to uphold, defend or persevere.

📖 Paul pays landscapers to *maintain* his grandfather's yard.

negotiate *v.* (ni-**goh**-shee-eyt): to settle an issue through discussion and compromise; to make an agreement by arranging a suitable deal; to successfully move or travel through something.

📖 Our director asked me to *negotiate* for more time to submit our grant to the state arts council.

objective *adj.* (*uh*b-**jek**-tiv): based on fact or actual observation through the five senses without personal opinion.
    n. a goal or purpose to be achieved.

📖 A rational, *objective* plan will convince protestors to listen to the board of education's *objective* in reducing teachers' health insurance.

partial *adj.* (**pahr**-sh*uh*l): relating to a section of something, not the whole thing; inclined to favor one thing over another; fond of someone or something.

 📖 Terrance is *partial* to vanilla ice cream cake over chocolate.

receive *v.* (ree-**seev**): to take into your possession; to acquire; to act as a receptacle or container; to accept or permit to enter.

 📖 Mr. Jones expects to *receive* a $2,500.00 tax refund from the IRS.

sameness *n.* (**saym**-nis): the quality of being just alike or identical without differences; uniformity.

 📖 The *sameness* of personality and preferences between identical twins can be a blessing and a curse.

territorial *adj.* (ter-i-**tohr**-ee-*uh* l): to be protective or defensive about an assigned area, especially against intruders.

 📖 Rena is very *territorial* about her desk and will confront anyone who tries to sit in her seat.

unbiased *adj.* (uhn-**bye**-*uh*st): free from prejudice; fair and objective; not showing favoritism or preference.

 📖 Lamar expected the principal to give an *unbiased* opinion about his behavior at a parent-teacher conference.

Vocabulary Exercise #2

Directions: Match the word from the left column to its correct definition on the right.

1. _____ kinetic

2. _____ latitude

3. _____ maintain

4. _____ negotiate

5. _____ objective

6. _____ partial

7. _____ receive

8. _____ sameness

9. _____ territorial

10. _____ unbiased

a) free from prejudice

b) active or lively

c) protective or defensive

d) a goal or purpose

e) to make a deal

f) to preserve

g) to take in

h) freedom from restrictions

i) not the whole thing

j) likeness or uniformity

Answers: Vocabulary Exercise #2

1. b

2. h

3. f

4. e

5. d

6. i

7. g

8. j

9. c

10. a

"You can suffocate a thought by expressing
it with too many words."
-- FRANK A. CLARK

absenteeism *n.* (ab-s*uh* n-**tee**-iz-*uh* m): missing for a long period
of time; chronic, multiple absences.

 📖 Candace got fired for tardiness and ***absenteeism***.

benevolent *adj.* (b*uh*-**nev**-*uh*-lu*h*nt): kind, generous; showing
good will.

 📖 My ***benevolent*** aunt created a scholarship fund for single parents.

carbon dioxide *n.* (***kahr***-*buh* n *dahy*-**ok**-*syde*): a colorless,
odorless gas that is naturally present in the atmosphere and
absorbed by plants for photosynthesis; also used in carbonated
beverages.

 📖 Clean air and ***carbon dioxide*** are essential to plant growth.

deception *n.* (dee-**sep**-sh*uh*n): the act or condition of being
tricked, lied to, misled or defrauded.

 📖 Mya's ***deception*** ended when the school called her parents about
 being absent from class.

earnest *adj.* (**ur**-nist): to be serious, focused and purposeful;
showing deep, heartfelt, sincere feelings; urgently important or
demanding attention.

 📖 The English teacher considered Heather's ***earnest*** request for a
 rewrite.

fascinating *adj.* (**fas**-*uh*-nay-ting): to be extremely interesting,
captivating or charming.

🕮 Partygoers surrounded the *fascinating* young woman and listened to her stories of worldwide travel all night long.

gore *n.* (gohr): blood, murder, violence, or gruesome details.

🕮 Zombie movies are filled with too much *gore* and wild savagery.

heedless *adj.* (**heed**-lis): careless, thoughtless, inconsiderate, or impulsive; not listening to instructions.

🕮 Being a *heedless* driver cost Lamont $2,500.00 in speeding tickets.

vague *adj.* (veyg): not clear; not directly stated or expressed; showing lack of clear perception or understanding.

🕮 The Dean made *vague* promises of faculty salary increases with no specified date for the raise.

weasel *n.* (**wee**-*zuh* l): a sneaky, untrustworthy or insincere person; a long, squirrel-like animal that mainly eats rodents.

v. to avoid a responsibility or an obligation.

🕮 Being the *weasel* that he is, Eddie tried to *weasel* his way out of paying back the money he borrowed from Yorka.

Vocabulary Exercise #3

Directions: Fill the blank with the correct word.

a) absenteeism   f) fascinating
b) benevolent   g) gore
c) carbon dioxide   h) heedless
d) deception   i) vague
e) earnest   j) weasel

1. Video games with too much _____can cause anxiety.

2. Terry's ideas were_____and unorganized.

3. Brian was_____and confident during his interview.

4. Constant_____can lead to mistrust or jail time.

5. A_____ran through my grandma's garden.

6. Dylan's grades dropped due to _____.

7. Plants need_____to live and grow.

8. Rachel's_____attempt to play basketball without complaining pleased her gym coach.

9. The kids played in the street_____to any possible danger.

10. Cara's_____attitude won her Employee of the Month.

Answers: Vocabulary Exercise #3

1. (g)—gore

2. (i) —vague

3. (f)—fascinating

4. (d)—deception

5. (j)—weasel

6. (a)—absenteeism

7. (c)—carbon dioxide

8. (e)—earnest

9. (h)—heedless

10. (b)—benevolent

Lesson Four

4

> "Colors fade, temples crumble, empires fall,
> but wise words endure."
> -- EDWARD THORNDIKE

immediately *adv.* (ih-**mee**-dee-it-lee): right now; instantly; without delay.

📖 The new mother *immediately* held her crying baby.

justify *v.* (**juhs**-*tuh*-fye): to defend, explain or rationalize an action, choice, thought or idea as ethical, honorable or noble; to prove something as right or reasonable; to declare as innocent or free from guilt.

📖 Politicians try to *justify* separating children from their parents by making immigration a crime.

legible *adj.* (**lej**-*uh*-*buh* l): able to read clearly or capable of being understood, especially handwriting or printed materials.

📖 If your employment application is not *legible*, it will get rejected.

matriarchy *n.* (**mey**-tree-ahr-kee): a society where women control political, social and economic structures; a social organization, family, community or clan where the mother is the head of household and descendants are traced through the mother's bloodline.

📖 Indonesia is home to the largest *matriarchy* in the world, since men often leave the country to seek other opportunities.

nurture *v.* (*ner-chur*): to support, protect, feed and educate, as in raising a child; to encourage growth and development.

📖 Randy and Paul bought their son a piano to *nurture* his interest in music.

obstruct *v.* (***uh**b*-struhkt): to block or close something to make it difficult to pass; to interrupt, hinder or oppose progress.

 📖 The tall trees *obstruct* my view of the lake from my balcony.

peer *n.* (**pee**-uhr): a person of equal rank to another either by age, social status, ability or qualifications; something of equal worth or quality.

 📖 High school students living in shelters formed a *peer* support group for other homeless teens.

reflection *n.* (ree-**flek**-sh*uh*n): the return of light or an image that appears on a surface, as in a mirror; careful consideration of something; an effect caused by an influence.

 📖 The rise of hate crimes is a reflection of our society's *racist* opinions.

sanitary *adj.* (**san**-uh-tare-ee): relating to cleanliness or health; free from dirt or bacteria.

 📖 Fast food workers must keep the kitchen *sanitary* at all times.

theory *n.* (**thee**-*uh*-ree): an idea, concept or abstract thought that has not been tested or proven as true, but formed by speculation; a scientifically acceptable rule or principle that guides research.

 📖 In *theory*, working four days a week should decrease company expenses, but in reality, doing so could cause staffing problems.

Vocabulary Exercise #4

Directions: Fill the blank with the correct word.

1. _____ to support and protect a child.

2. _____ an unproven idea.

3. _____ right now.

4. _____ a female society.

5. _____ a person of the same age as another.

6. _____ to block something.

7. _____ free from dirt.

8. _____ easy to read.

9. _____ a mirror image.

10. _____ to defend or explain.

Answers: Vocabulary Exercise #4

1. nurture

2. theory

3. immediately

4. matriarchy

5. peer

6. obstruct

7. sanitary

8. legible

9. reflection

10. justify

"When a man eats his words, that's recycling."
-- FRANK A. CLARK

abstract *adj.* (*ab*-strakt): not easily understood; not a true representation of reality; impersonal or detached.

> *n.* (*ab*-strakt): a short summary of a longer written document, such as a research report or scientific study.

📖 The artist drew *abstract* representations of people without faces.

bewilder *v.* (bee-**will**-duhr): to confuse, surprise, baffle, astonish or dumbfound.

📖 Today's young women *bewilder* me with their lack of modesty.

category *n.* (**kat**-i-gohr-ee): a smaller group, class or division from a larger whole.

📖 Cardi B won the Grammy music *category* for best rap album.

decompose *v.* (dee-k*uh*m-**poze**): to break down or disintegrate; to rot or decay.

📖 As dead animal bodies *decompose*, the smell becomes unbearable.

economic *adj.* (ee-k*uh*-nom-ik): related to the production, distribution and purchase of goods and services; pertaining to personal resources of money.

📖 Dori had to drop out of college for *economic* reasons.

fiction *n.* (**fik**-sh*uh*n): an invented or made-up story from the imagination; a class of literature based on creative, imagined stories, such as novels or short stories.

📖 The late Toni Morrison's *fiction* features the struggles and successes of everyday African American people.

governance *n.* (**guhv**-er-n*uh*nce): a system of authority, management and control; government.

    📖 The university president created a new plan of ***governance*** that severely limited faculty input.

uneventful *adj.* (uhn-ee-**vent**-f*uh*l): boring, not exciting; routine or humdrum; nothing interesting or noteworthy.

    📖 Brenda spent another ***uneventful*** weekend eating fast food and binge watching her favorite shows.

variation *n.* (vair-ee-**ey**-sh*uh*n): an instance of change; something that displays slight differences or noticeable changes.

    📖 United States medical officers continue to deny any ***variation*** in childhood vaccines from the 1970s until now.

wholesome *adj.* (**hohl**-s*uh*m): beneficial or healthy; promoting health and well-being.

    📖 Exercise and ***wholesome*** food can lower high blood pressure.

Vocabulary Exercise #5

Directions: Choose the correct definition.

1. economic

    a) abundance
    b) scarcity
    c) money

2. uneventful

    a) exciting
    b) boring
    c) unpleasant

3. category

    a) a story
    b) a summary
    c) a division

4. governance

    a) authority and control
    b) hostility and violence
    c) supervision and work

5. variation

    a) likeness
    b) difference
    c) satisfaction

6. bewilder

   a) to confuse
   b) to motivate
   c) to understand

7. fiction

   a) true
   b) made up
   c) serious

8. abstract

   a) a book
   b) a report
   c) a summary

9. wholesome

   a) healthy
   b) sickly
   c) reliable

10. decompose

    a) to increase
    b) to live
    c) to rot

Answers on the back of this page.

Answers: Vocabulary Exercise #5

1. c

2. b

3. c

4. a

5. b

6. a

7. b

8. c

9. a

10. c

Your Score

_____ correct out of 10

10 – 100%
9 – 90%
8 – 80%
7 – 70%
6 – 60%
5 – 50%
4 – 40%
3 – 30%
2 – 20%
1 – 10%

100%........Excellent
90-80%......Good
70%..........Fair
60%..........Keep Practicing

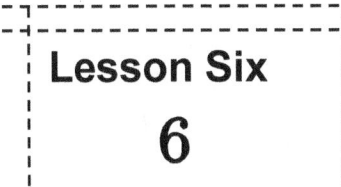

Lesson Six

6

"If there is a book that you want to read,
but it hasn't been written yet,
you must be the one to write it."
-- TONI MORRISON

hierarchy *n.* (**hahy**-*uh*-rahr-kee): a system that ranks one person or thing above another; the classification of a group of people by economic, social or professional status.

📖 The company's management *hierarchy* made it almost impossible for entry level workers to get promoted in less than five years.

imperialism *n.* (im-**peer**-ee-*uh*-liz-*uh* m): the general expansion of authority, power and influence; a government or empire's policy of extending its rule over other foreign countries or nations by taking over all or part of their physical, economic or social structures.

📖 Through American *imperialism*, the United States annexed Hawaii and took control of its trade ports and harbors.

liberation *n.* (lib-*uh*-**ray**-sh*uh* n): freedom; the state of being free or liberated; the act of gaining social, economic or equal human rights for a group of people.

📖 The *liberation* of black South Africans from apartheid created a new atmosphere of democracy.

mandate *n.* (**man**-deyt): a command from a higher authority; an obligatory or forced requirement.

📖 A *mandate* from the Supreme Court banned abortions in 48 states.

obvious *adj.* (**ob**-*vee-uhs*): plainly evident; easily seen, recognized or understood.

📖 Chocolate and vanilla were two *obvious* choices at the yogurt shop.

persistent *adj.* (per-**sis**-t*uh*nt): existing for a long time; lasting or enduring despite interference, obstacles or treatment.

📖 Charles finally had to see a doctor about his ***persistent*** cough.

reliable *adj.* (ree-**lye**-*uh*-b*uh*l): trustworthy or accurate; dependable; giving the same result time after time.

📖 Teresa needed ***reliable*** transportation to commute to her new job 45 minutes away.

scornful *adj.* (**skohrn**-f*uh* l): full of contempt or criticism; rude and disrespectful.

📖 Chad mocked the teacher with a ***scornful*** grin and rude gestures before security removed him from the classroom.

thorough *adj.* (**thur**-oh): utterly complete; extremely focused on accuracy and detail; painstaking and careful about details.

📖 The doctor performed a ***thorough*** examination on Michael before giving a diagnosis.

variety *n.* (v*uh*-**rahy**-i-tee): several different types of things; an assortment.

📖 Continental breakfast at the hotel consisted of a small ***variety*** of donuts and orange juice.

Vocabulary Exercise #6

Directions: Match the word from the left column to its correct definition on the right.

1. ____ hierarchy

2. ____ imperialism

3. ____ liberation

4. ____ mandate

5. ____ obvious

6. ____ persistent

7. ____ reliable

8. ____ scornful

9. ____ thorough

10. ____ variety

a) plainly evident

b) full of contempt

c) an assortment

d) utterly complete

e) a ranking system

f) dependable

g) expansion of power

h) long lasting

i) authoritative command

j) freedom

Answers: Vocabulary Exercise #6

1. e

2. g

3. j

4. i

5. a

6. h

7. f

8. b

9. d

10. c

Your Score

_____ correct out of 10

10 – 100%
9 – 90%
8 – 80%
7 – 70%
6 – 60%
5 – 50%
4 – 40%
3 – 30%
2 – 20%
1 – 10%

100%........Excellent
90-80%......Good
70%..........Fair
60%..........Keep Practicing

"Be careful of your thoughts; they may
become words at any moment."
-- IARA GASSEN

accommodation(s) *n.* (*uh*-kom-*uh*-**dey**-sh*uh* n): something that is provided for convenience or to satisfy a need; adjustments; lodging, food and services related to traveling, usually stated in *accommodations*.

📖 The *accommodations* in this hotel include free high-speed internet.

bias *n.* (**bye**-*uh*s): a personal outlook, feeling, tendency or opinion that is based on prejudice or unreasonable information.

📖 Racial *bias* toward Black teenagers send innocent young people to the grave before their time.

certification *n.* (sur-t*uh*-fi-**kay**-sh*uh* n): confirmation; recognition that special qualifications have been met.

📖 Most public schools will not hire education graduates without teacher *certification*.

degradation *n.* (deg-r*uh*-**day**-sh*uh*n): the act or process of wearing down or declining to a low state.

📖 The *degradation* of moral and spiritual values causes chaos in society.

ecosystem *n.* (*eek*-oh-sis-tuh m): a system or group of connected elements formed by the interaction of a community of organisms with their environment; any system or network of interconnecting and interacting parts, as in business.

📖 Pastors, members, volunteers and other spiritual leaders form the human *ecosystem* of a successful church.

figurative *adj.* (**fig**-yer-*uh*-tiv): not literal; expressed by figures of speech or metaphors; represented by a likeness, emblem or resemblance.

 📖 Even after her retirement, English faculty at Morehouse College still regarded Dr. E. Delores Stephens as the ***figurative*** head of the department.

greenhouse *n.* (**green**-hawse): a building or room, usually made of glass, that is set at a certain temperature to protect the growth of plants.

 📖 The ***greenhouse*** in my grandpa's backyard was filled with tomatoes and vegetables that were out of season.

humanitarian *adj.* (hyoo-man-i-**tair**-ee-*uh* n): having concern for the welfare and happiness of people.

 n. a person that helps others through service or by promoting social reforms to improve the lives of other people.

 📖 The singer Bono of the band *U2* is well-known for his ***humanitarian*** efforts around the world.

impetuous *adj.* (im-**pech**-oo-*uh*s): related to sudden action without thinking; impulsive or passionate emotion; moving with great force.

 📖 The child's ***impetuous*** running around the store forced his mother to leave without buying anything.

withdrawal *n.* (with-**draw**-*uh* l): the act of removing something or taking something back, social or emotional detachment.

 📖 Lena's ***withdrawal*** of $500 from her checking account caused a negative balance.

Vocabulary Exercise #7

Directions: Fill the blank with the correct word.

a) accommodations   f) figurative

b) bias   g) greenhouse

c) certification   h) humanitarian

d) degradation   i) impetuous

e) ecosystem   j) withdrawal

1. Myron's _____decision to quit his job angered his wife.

2. The club owner's_____against heavy set women caused a lawsuit.

3. Google Adwords_____can increase employment options.

4. Some students need special_____to complete their assessments.

5. A good novel includes_____language.

6. Cannabis can be grown all year in a_____.

7. Even the best_____efforts cannot eliminate poverty.

8. A _____of the brakes caused the car to crash.

9. Early_____from a retirement account will incur penalties.

10. The ocean's_____regulates sea life without intervention.

Answers: Vocabulary Exercise #7

1. i—impetuous

2. b—bias

3. c—certification

4. a—accommodations

5. f—figurative

6. g—greenhouse

7. h—humanitarian

8. d—degradation

9. j—withdrawal

10. e—ecosystem

"When you take stuff from one writer,
it's plagiarism, but when you take it
from many writers, it's research."
-- WILSON MIZNER

---

accurate *adj.* (**ak**-yer-it): free from errors or mistakes; exact.

📖 Check to make sure your pay hours for this week are ***accurate***.

brainstorming *n.* (**breyn**-stowr-ming): a group problem-solving technique where members use creative thinking to develop new ideas.

📖 ***Brainstorming*** is good for group projects.

license *n.* (**lye**-s*uh* ns): a certificate, tag, plate or other document that gives permission to do something or to conduct business; permission to act; freedom allowed in special situations.

📖 Not all states require a ***license*** to carry a gun.

maximum *n.* (**mak**-s*uh*-m*uh* m): the greatest amount possible; an upper limit allowed by law or regulation.

📖 The credit card ***maximum*** for ATM withdrawals is $500 per day.

omnipotent *adj.* (*om-**nip**-uh-tuhnt*): almighty; having great or unlimited power, authority or influence.

📖 Despite what the president or world leaders might think, only God is ***omnipotent***.

pincushion *n.* (**pin**-k*uh* sh-*uh* n): a soft object where pins are stuck, especially for sewing.

📖 My grandmother used a throw pillow as a ***pincushion*** while altering my sister's wedding dress.

reluctant *adj.* (ree-**luhk**-t*uh*nt): feeling or showing hesitation or unwillingness.

📖 Damian was ***reluctant*** to get in the car with his troubled cousins.

seminar *n.* (**sem**-*uh*-nahr): a scheduled meeting for teaching, learning and exchanging information followed by discussion; a small group of scholarly students engaged in advanced study.

📖 Professor Hampton's grant writing ***seminar*** was very informative.

tiny *adj.* (**tye**-nee): very small.

📖 A ***tiny*** speck of sand irritated my eye for hours.

verify *v.* (**ver**-*uh*-fahy): to make certain; to establish the truth or accuracy of something.

📖 The reporter had to ***verify*** the caller's story before telling the editor.

Vocabulary Exercise #8

Directions: Fill the blank with the correct word.

1. _____very small.

2. _____a soft object.

3. _____the highest amount.

4. _____showing hesitation.

5. _____permission to do something.

6. _____ to make certain.

7. _____all powerful.

8. _____a problem-solving technique.

9. _____without errors or mistakes.

10. _____a teaching and learning session.

Answers: Vocabulary Exercise #8

1. tiny

2. pincushion

3. maximum

4. reluctant

5. license

6. verify

7. omnipotent

8. brainstorming

9. accurate

10. seminar

"Fools live to regret their words,
wise men to regret their silence."
-- WILL HENRY

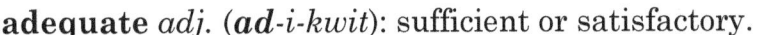

adequate *adj.* (***ad***-*i*-*kwit*): sufficient or satisfactory.

📖 Without ***adequate*** lighting, the video will appear dark and fuzzy.

brandish *v.* (**bran**-dish): to shake or wave in an aggressive manner.

📖 Mental illness caused a disturbed man to ***brandish*** a gun in Wal-Mart.

citizen *n.* (**sit**-*uh*-*zuh* n): a person or native born in a particular city, state or country who deserves protection as its member or inhabitant; a resident or inhabitant.

📖 Any ***citizen*** of the United States can apply for college.

deliberate *adj.* (dih-**lib**-er-it): intentional or on purpose; carefully considered; slow, unhurried and steady in allowing time to make a decision.

> **deliberate** *v.* (dih-**lib**-er-ate): taking time to think carefully about something and to consider the consequences.

📖 Deborah made a ***deliberate*** decision to ***deliberate*** on adopting a baby.

effect *n.* (**ee**-fekt): the end result of an action; a consequence; power to influence or to produce results.

> **effect** *v.* (ih-**fekt**): to make something happen; to produce a result; to put into operation.

📖 The positive ***effect*** of the *Black Lives Matter* movement is the awareness that we all must ***effect*** change in racially biased systems.

filthy *adj.* (**fill**-thee): very dirty; disgusting, foul or vulgar.

📖 The *filthy*, abandoned house was overrun with rats.

hypothesis *n.* (hi-**poth**-*uh*-sis): an assumption, idea or a guess that tries to explain something, but needs further investigation or research to prove that it is true.

📖 According to Mark's *hypothesis*, his jilted ex-girlfriend stole his car as payback for their broken engagement.

inclement *adj.* (in-**klem**-*uh* nt): severe, rough, harsh or stormy (as in the weather); extreme in temper or action.

📖 Due to heavy sleet and snow, the *inclement* weather policy will take effect for all school districts in the city.

lobby *n.* (**lah**-bee): a small area or an entrance hall connected to a larger space that serves as a waiting room; a group of people that work to influence the votes of government officials in favor of the group's special interests.

v. to try to influence the votes of public or government officials.

📖 In the *lobby* of the state capitol, charter school advocates tried to *lobby* incoming legislators to increase their school funding.

metaphorical *adj.* (me-tuh-**fòr**-ah-kuhl): symbolic; not literal; related to the descriptive figure of speech that does not use the words *"like"* or *"as."*

📖 Jimmy gave Renaye a *metaphorical* wedding ring made of aluminum foil since they were broke college students.

Vocabulary Exercise #9

Directions: Choose the correct definition for each word.

1. metaphorical

    a) literal
    b) symbolic
    c) false

2. citizen

    a) a foreigner
    b) a ruler
    c) a native

3. effect

    a) a result
    b) a direction
    c) a cause

4. brandish

    a) to fight
    b) to intimidate
    c) to wave violently

5. filthy

    a) clean
    b) dirty
    c) funny

6. adequate

   a) limited
   b) sufficient
   c) steady

7. inclement

   a) mild
   b) friendly
   c) severe

8. lobby

   a) to talk
   b) to influence
   c) to hire

9. hypothesis

   a) a statement
   b) a conclusion
   c) a guess

10. deliberate

   a) accidental
   b) intentional
   c) incredible

Answers on the back of this page.

Sign up for **"Public Speaking Skills & Drills"** at www.arhampton.com/classes.

Answers: Vocabulary Exercise #9

1. b—symbolic

2. c—a native

3. a—result

4. c—to wave violently

5. b—dirty

6. b—sufficient

7. c—severe

8. b—to influence

9. c—a guess

10. b—intentional

Your Score

_____ correct out of 10

10 – 100%
9 – 90%
8 – 80%
7 – 70%
6 – 60%
5 – 50%
4 – 40%
3 – 30%
2 – 20%
1 – 10%

100%........Excellent
90-80%......Good
70%..........Fair
60%..........Keep Practicing

"The most valuable of all talents is that of never using two words when one will do."

-- THOMAS JEFFERSON

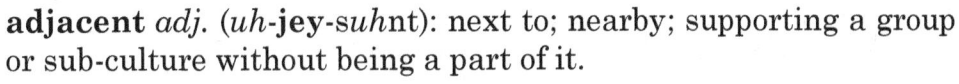

adjacent *adj.* (*uh*-**jey**-su*h*nt): next to; nearby; supporting a group or sub-culture without being a part of it.

    📖 The *adjacent* to the back door of the house.

brogue *n.* (brōhg): a heavy leather shoe with decorative stitching derived from Ireland; an Irish accent; any strong regional accent.

    📖 The *brogue* of the black, Scottish YouTube star made her speech difficult to understand.

coalition *n.* (koh-*uh*-**lish**-*uh*n): a group forming a temporary union or alliance; a combination or fusion.

    📖 In the 1960s and 1970s, *The Rainbow **Coalition*** included ethnic community groups of different races to fight injustice in Chicago.

delicate *adj.* (**del**-ah-kit): easy to break or damage; fragile or frail; weak or sickly; pleasing to the taste or smell in a subtle, mild way.

    📖 The *delicate*, gold bracelet snapped when Hannah tried to fasten it around her wrist.

emotion *n.* (*ih*-**moh**-*shuh* n): an experience of strong feelings, such as joy, sorrow, love, pain, anger, peace, etc.

    📖 Do not make important decisions based on *emotion*, but use logic to choose wisely.

flight *n.* (flaīhyt): the ability to fly; a scheduled trip by airplane; the act of running away; an imaginative, brilliant or unrestrained activity.

📖 Chad's *flight* to London got delayed for two hours due to bad weather.

incredible *adj.* (in-**kred**-*uh*-b*uh*l): hard to believe; amazing; so extraordinary it seems impossible.

📖 Simone Biles' *incredible* triple-double dismount during the 2019 *U.S. Gymnastics Championships* was jaw-dropping.

lyre *n.* (lahy*uh* r): a musical instrument with strings from ancient Greece that resembles a small, U-shaped harp.

📖 The orchestra performed Handel's *Passacaglia* with a harp and a *lyre*.

method *n.* (**meth**-*uh*d): a process, procedure or technique for getting something done in a particular way or manner; an orderly sequence or plan.

📖 The Martha Graham *method* of modern dance resembles ballet.

onerous *adj.* (**oh**-ner *uh*s): causing heavy hardship or burden; oppressive.

📖 The *onerous* admissions process kept many first-generation students from applying to college.

Vocabulary Exercise #10

Directions: Match the word from the left column to its correct definition on the right.

1. ____ adjacent

2. ____ brogue

3. ____ coalition

4. ____ delicate

5. ____ emotion

6. ____ flight

7. ____ incredible

8. ____ lyre

9. ____ method

10. ____ onerous

a) fragile or frail

b) strong feelings

c) next to

d) a heavy accent

e) causing hardship

f) a musical instrument

g) a process or procedure

h) ability to fly

i) a temporary union

j) hard to believe

Answers: Vocabulary Exercise #10

1. c

2. d

3. i

4. a

5. b

6. h

7. j

8. f

9. g

10. e

Your Score

_____ correct out of 10

10 – 100%
9 – 90%
8 – 80%
7 – 70%
6 – 60%
5 – 50%
4 – 40%
3 – 30%
2 – 20%
1 – 10%

100%........Excellent
90-80%......Good
70%...........Fair
60%...........Keep Practicing

"There is no greater agony than bearing
an untold story inside you."
-- MAYA ANGELOU

poll *n.* (pōhl): a collection of opinions on a particular subject that are later analyzed in order to make a decision; a place to cast a vote for an election.

> **poll** *v.* (pōhl): to question or survey people on a particular subject and record their answers.

> 📖 According to my social media ***poll***, people think I should wear plum colored lipstick instead of red.

remedy *n.* (**rem**-uh-dee): something that cures or relieves a disease, sickness or ailment; a healing medicine or treatment.

> **remedy** *v.* (**rem**-uh-dee): to cure, heal or relieve; to correct or make something right, (as in a situation).

> 📖 My grandma tells us to drink ginger ale to ***remedy*** a stomach ache.

sincere *adj.* (sin-**seer**): to be honest and truthful; genuine or real.

> 📖 Ken made a ***sincere*** attempt to see his daughter perform, but he missed the show because of traffic delays.

tolerable *adj.* (**tol**-er-*uh*-b*uh*l): capable of being endured; fairly good, not that bad.

> 📖 Vegan burgers are ***tolerable***, but not tasty.

admonish *v.* (*ad*-**mon**-*ish*): to warn, to caution or advise against something; to mildly scold, fuss or lecture.

> 📖 I ***admonish*** you to submit your essay early to avoid failing this class.

biodiversity *n.* (bahy-oh-di-**vur**-si-tee): biological variety in an environment as indicated by the numbers of different species of plants and animals.

    📖 The *biodiversity* in the Amazon rain forest includes over 10,000 species of wildlife.

collective *n.* (k*uh*-**lek**-tiv): a group of people with shared responsibilities and opinions that act as one body; a business or enterprise that is owned and operated by members of a group.

    collective *adj.* (k*uh*-**lek**-tiv): related to a group of people; considered as one whole; shared by all members of the group.

    📖 The class reported the demanding professor in a *collective* complaint to the Dean.

demanding *adj.* (dee-**man**-ding): calling for intense effort or attention; requiring more than is needed.

    📖 The *demanding* professor received complaints about harsh grading.

enamored *adj.* (ih-**nam**-erd): strongly interested or fascinated; to be filled with love or passion.

    📖 *Enamored* with her work, Raymond paid for my sister's art studio.

frugal *adj.* (**froo**-g*uh* l): cheap; inexpensive; not wasteful; using few resources.

    📖 As newlyweds, Janice did not appreciate her husband's budgeting and *frugal* spending habits.

Vocabulary Exercise #11

Directions: Write the word for each definition in the space provided.

1. requiring more effort

2. honest and genuine

3. to question or survey

4. to warn against something

5. strongly interested or fascinated

6. cheap or inexpensive

7. variety of species

8. a cure or treatment

9. a group of people

10. not that bad

Answers: Vocabulary Exercise #11

1. demanding

2. sincere

3. poll

4. admonish

5. enamored

6. frugal

7. biodiversity

8. remedy

9. collective

10. tolerable

Lesson Twelve

12

"Putting words on paper regularly is part of the necessary discipline of writing."
-- PEARL CLEAGE

affect *n.* (*af*-ekt): a feeling or emotion; an observed emotional response.

> **affect** *v.* (*uh-fekt*): to act on; to influence; to produce a change in something.

> 📖 The medicine's *affect* on Tyra's mood began to *affect* how she talked to people.

communicate *v.* (k*uh*-**myoo**-ni-keyt): to express thoughts, feelings or information easily and effectively through speech, writing or nonverbal methods like drawing or body language.

> 📖 The director wrote a memo to *communicate* his displeasure with the staff's performance.

deplete *v.* (dih-**pleet**): to empty or exhaust; to seriously decrease an abundant supply.

> 📖 Working too much can *deplete* your energy.

indifferent *adj.* (in-**dif**-er-*uh*nt): not caring; showing no interest or concern; impartial with no bias, prejudice or preference.

> 📖 The one-year-old was *indifferent* about her first birthday party.

microscope *n.* (**mahy**-kr*uh*-skohp): an optical instrument with a magnifying lens that enlarges objects too small to see with the natural eye.

> 📖 The doctor used a *microscope* to see the bacteria on Ted's skin cells.

oppressive *adj.* (*uh*-**pres**-iv): excessively harsh, distressing or burdensome.

📖 The *oppressive* heat dried the farmers' fields and caused a drought.

possess *v.* (p*uh*-**zes**): to own; to occupy, dominate or control.

📖 Sheila wanted to *possess* her boyfriend's love by paying for his car.

renew *v.* (ri-**noo**): to restore or replenish; to start again; to get an extension.

📖 Remind Kim to *renew* her library card before the end of the month.

solicitude *n.* (s*uh*-**lis**-i-tood): anxiety or concern; an attitude of excessive care and concern.

📖 Ramona's *solicitude* over her daughter's first menstrual cycle made the girl uncomfortable.

transaction *n.* (tran-**zak**-sh*uh*n): a process where something is exchanged or transferred, such as products, services or money; a beneficial arrangement between two or more people.

📖 The real estate *transaction* between Sarah and her ex-husband fell through when the owner raised the price.

Vocabulary Exercise #12

Directions: Choose the correct meaning.

1. indifferent

    a) different
    b) unconcerned
    c) biased

2. possess

    a) to own
    b) to exchange
    c) to respect

3. deplete

    a) to exhaust
    b) to fill
    c) to renew

4. communicate

    a) to promote
    b) to breathe
    c) to talk

5. oppressive

    a) depressed
    b) harsh
    c) angry

6. transaction

    a) an interaction
    b) an email
    c) an exchange

7. renew

    a) to restore
    b) to stop
    c) to arrive

8. affect

    a) to scold
    b) to change
    c) to receive

9. solicitude

    a) anxiety
    b) depression
    c) responsibility

10. microscope

    a) a weapon
    b) a magnifying instrument
    c) a clamp

Answers on the back of this page.

Answers: Vocabulary Exercise #12

1. b—unconcerned

2. a—to own

3. a—to exhaust

4. c—to talk

5. b—harsh

6. c—an exchange

7. a—to restore

8. b—to change

9. a—anxiety

10. b—a magnifying instrument

Your Score

_____ correct out of 10

10 – 100%
9 – 90%
8 – 80%
7 – 70%
6 – 60%
5 – 50%
4 – 40%
3 – 30%
2 – 20%
1 – 10%

100%........Excellent
90-80%......Good
70%...........Fair
60%...........Keep Practicing

"A writer should get as much education as possible, but just going to school is not enough; if it were, all owners of doctorates would be inspired writers." – GWENDOLYN BROOKS

agenda *n.* (*uh*-**jen**-duh): a list or an outline of things to be completed or considered.

📖 The student body president passed out an ***agenda*** of new business items to all of the committee members at the meeting.

concentration *n.* (kon-s*uh*n-**tray**-sh*uh*n): intense attention or mental focus; an academic major or an area of focus within that major; something that is condensed or collected into one body, mass or force.

📖 An athlete performs poorly when his or her ***concentration*** is broken.

deposit *v.* (dih-**poz**-it): to submit something or to place something for safekeeping, such as in a bank; to give a partial payment.

> **deposit** *n.* (dih-**poz**-it): money that is put in a bank; something given as a partial payment.

📖 Teresa wanted to ***deposit*** money into her account, but the bank would not accept a large cash ***deposit*** after 2 p.m.

encourage *v.* (en-**kur**-ij): to inspire or to offer support; to persuade or urge; to promote, advance or cause something to happen.

📖 Mrs. Divers loves to ***encourage*** her kindergarten class to sing songs.

frustration *n.* (fruh-**stray**-sh*uh*n): a feeling of impatience or dissatisfaction; something that is hindered or interrupted.

📖 After four unsuccessful attempts to call the doctor to the office, the assistant's ***frustration*** turned into anger.

indignant *adj.* (in-**dig**-n*uh*nt): filled with strong displeasure or anger at something that is considered offensive or insulting.

    📖 The drunken soldier's ***indignant*** remark to a pregnant African American lady fueled a Twitter outrage.

minimum *n.* (**min**-*uh*-m*uh* m): the lowest possible amount.

    📖 Derricka needs to maintain a ***minimum*** 3.0 GPA to keep her scholarship.

organic *adj.* (ore-**gan**-ik): formed naturally; grown or farmed without chemicals; related to plants, animals or living organisms.

    📖 You can buy ***organic*** fruit and vegetables from local farmers instead of grocery stores.

potential *n.* (p*uh*-**ten**-sh*uh* l): a possibility; hidden talents or abilities that are not fully developed.

    📖 All children are born with the ***potential*** to live a successful life.

renewal *n.* (ri-**noo**-*uh* l): something that is restored, refreshed, revived or made new again; an extension.

    📖 After 10 years of marriage, Nadia planned a vow ***renewal*** ceremony.

Vocabulary Exercise #13

Directions: Choose the correct synonym or similar meaning.

1. renewal

    a) return
    b) refreshed
    c) organic

2. frustration

    a) satisfaction
    b) anger
    c) dissatisfaction

3. minimum

    a) highest
    b) lowest
    c) medium

4. agenda

    a) a list
    b) a book
    c) a song

5. potential

    a) unavailable
    b) possibility
    c) awareness

6. concentration

    a) distraction

    b) maturity

    c) focus

7. indignant

    a) strong displeasure

    b) frustration

    c) inferior

8. deposit

    a) payment

    b) tuition

    c) withdrawal

9. organic

    a) spicy

    b) mild

    c) natural

10. encourage

    a) unavailable

    b) urge

    c) impatient

Answers on the back of this page.

Answers: Vocabulary Exercise #13

1. b

2. c

3. b

4. a

5. b

6. c

7. a

8. a

9. c

10. b

<table>
<tr><td colspan="2">Your Score</td></tr>
<tr><td colspan="2">_____ correct out of 10</td></tr>
<tr><td>10 – 100%</td><td></td></tr>
<tr><td>9 – 90%</td><td></td></tr>
<tr><td>8 – 80%</td><td></td></tr>
<tr><td>7 – 70%</td><td></td></tr>
<tr><td>6 – 60%</td><td></td></tr>
<tr><td>5 – 50%</td><td></td></tr>
<tr><td>4 – 40%</td><td></td></tr>
<tr><td>3 – 30%</td><td></td></tr>
<tr><td>2 – 20%</td><td></td></tr>
<tr><td>1 – 10%</td><td></td></tr>
<tr><td>100%........Excellent</td><td></td></tr>
<tr><td>90-80%......Good</td><td></td></tr>
<tr><td>70%..........Fair</td><td></td></tr>
<tr><td>60%..........Keep Practicing</td><td></td></tr>
</table>

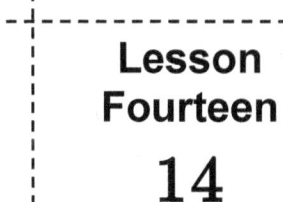

Lesson Fourteen

14

"Words mean more than what is set down on paper. It takes the human voice to infuse them with deeper meaning." — MAYA ANGELOU

aggravate *v.* (**ag**-r*uh*-veyt): to make worse, more serious or more severe; to make angry.

📖 The trainer told Shawn not to **aggravate** his knee injury.

concern *n.* (k*uh*n-**surn**): a problem or issue; an uneasy feeling of uncertainty and apprehension; to involve or include.

📖 The manager listened to the employees' **concerns** and made changes.

despicable *adj.* (**des**-pi-k*uh*-b*uh*l): distasteful or disgusting; mean or obnoxious.

📖 Mona's **despicable** husband constantly insults her appearance.

engrossing *adj.* (en-**grow**-sing): all consuming or absorbing; fully occupying your attention, thoughts, and focus.

📖 The novel was so **engrossing** that Marco did not eat until he finished reading it.

fungus *n.* (**fuhn**-*guh s*): a spongy, abnormal growth that can occur from mold, mildew, mushrooms, rust or yeast that can develop into a chronic infection on the skin.

    fungi *n.* (**fuhn**-*guy*) plural form of fungus.

📖 Because shoes and socks get wet and sweaty, foot **fungus** is a big problem for many athletes.

industrial *adj.* (in-**duhs**-tree-*uh* l): describing or related to workers, labor, manufacturing or a collection of money-making businesses; hardworking or steady.

 📖 Phillip's *industrial* pursuit of broadcasting led to a career in radio.

modern *adj.* (**mah**-dern): related to current, present day times, not the past.

 📖 Women and girl's *modern* fashion choices are often short, skimpy and inappropriate for public display.

organism *n.* (**ohr**-g*uh*-niz-*uh*m): a form of life that grows and maintains vital processes; a complex organization or system with separate parts that acts as a whole and resembles a living being.

 📖 The state department of education is an *organism* that feeds on disruption, disorganization and personal bias.

poverty *n.* (**pah**-vur-tee): a condition of being poor with little or no money, support or resources; a state of deficiency or insufficiency.

 📖 Their efforts to assist 1,000 students was frustrated by a *poverty* of donations.

solve *v.* (saulv): to clear up, explain or find the answer.

 📖 Kim and her supervisor used video cameras to *solve* the problem of missing office supplies.

Vocabulary Exercise #14

Directions: Match the word from the left column to its correct definition on the right.

1. ____ modern

2. ____ concern

3. ____ fungus

4. ____ aggravate

5. ____ industrial

6. ____ solve

7. ____ engrossing

8. ____ organism

9. ____ despicable

10. ____ poverty

a) to make worse

b) being poor

c) distasteful or mean

d) find the answer

e) a problem or issue

f) related to workers

g) all consuming

h) present day

i) a life form

j) a growth

Answers: Vocabulary Exercise #14

1. h

2. e

3. j

4. a

5. f

6. d

7. g

8. i

9. c

10. b

Lesson Fifteen

15

"You don't start out writing good stuff. You start out writing crap and thinking it's good stuff, and then gradually you get better at it." -- OCTAVIA E. BUTLER

replace *v.* (ri-**plays**): to substitute; to restore, return or make good.

📖 The janitor had to *replace* the old microwave in the break room with a new one.

statistics *n.* (st*u*h-**tis**-tiks): the branch of mathematics that deals with the collection, analysis and interpretation of numerical data; facts and information that include numbers.

📖 *Statistics* show that 80% of black families are led by single mothers.

agile *adj.* (**aj**-*ahyl*): quick, active, lively, flexible and well-coordinated in the movement of the body or thoughts of the mind.

📖 The spirited dance routine of the *agile* ice skater impressed the audience and the judges.

conscious *adj.* (**kon**-sh*uh*s): to be awake, alert and fully aware of your inner self and your external environment.

📖 Meditation quiets the *conscious* activity of the mind.

determine *v.* (dih-**tur**-min): to settle or decide something, such as a dispute; to conclude through reasoning or observation.

📖 The police could not *determine* the suspect's innocence without a lie detector test.

attorney *n.* (*uh*-**tur**-*nee*): a person who is legally assigned to conduct business on behalf of another person, usually a lawyer.

📖 Carla and Sam hired an *attorney* to file for bankruptcy.

infection *n.* (in-**fek**-sh*uh* n): something that is contaminated with a disease or bacteria; a sore, rash or other ailment caused by the transfer of disease or bacteria.

    📖 The flu is a viral *infection* that could become deadly if untreated.

modulate *v.* (**moj**-*uh*-leyt): to soften or tone down; to adjust the volume of something, especially the voice or music; to adapt to fit certain situations.

    📖 Anthony had to *modulate* his normal speaking voice to be heard in the large auditorium.

originate *v.* (*uh*-**rij**-*uh*-neyt): to have started or begun from something; to be born from, initiate or give rise to.

    📖 Rappers *originate* from hip-hop street culture.

practical *adj.* (**prak**-ti-k*uh*l): to be useful, realistic or sensible, especially for everyday work or ordinary activities.

    📖 Buy a *practical* wedding gift like silverware or pots and pans.

Vocabulary Exercise #15

Directions: Fill the blank with the correct word.

a) replace   f) attorney
b) statistics   g) infection
c) agile   h) modulate
d) conscious   i) originate
e) determine   j) practical

1. Tires cost too much money to _____at one time.

2. A judge will_____the cost for damages.

3. Surveys and polls are used to gather_____.

4. Coffee beans_____from Africa.

5. I did not need an_____for traffic court.

6. Antibiotics cleared Tanya's _____.

7. Ella needs to wear_____shoes instead of high heels.

8. My 90-year-old grandmother's mind and sense of humor are still_____.

9. Tell Simon to_____his performance for the kids.

10. Teens need to be more_____of their surroundings.

Answers: Vocabulary Exercise #15

1. a—replace

2. e—determine

3. b—statistics

4. i—originate

5. f—attorney

6. g—infection

7. j—practical

8. c—agile

9. h—modulate

10. d—conscious

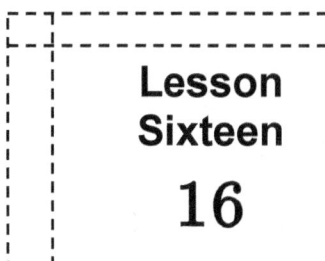

Lesson Sixteen

16

"Words are like weapons; they wound sometimes."

-- CHER

replacement *n.* (ri-**pleys**-m*uh* nt): a person or object that substitutes for or takes the place of something else.

📖 Mr. Morgan's hip *replacement* surgery was successful.

strident *adj.* (**streyed**-nt): having a shrill, irritating quality or character; making a harsh sound; grating or creaking.

📖 Tamika's *strident* laugh made the dog run outside.

allow *v.* (*uh*-*lau*): to give permission or to permit; to assign as a share or suitable amount (i.e. allow for).

📖 These luxury apartments do not *allow* pets of any kind.

consumer *n.* (k*uh* n-**soo**-mer): a person or organization that uses a product or service like a customer.

📖 Fast food industries want *consumers* to keep eating for convenience instead of health.

develop *v.* (*dih*-*vel*-*uh* p): to grow or expand; to grow into an advanced or mature state; to bring out the capabilities or possibilities.

📖 My parents watched me *develop* into a college-educated, responsible young woman, despite my wild teen years.

enhance *v.* (en-**hans**): to highlight, intensify, magnify or raise to a higher level; to make more attractive or valuable.

📖 Take a writing course to ***enhance*** your job opportunities.

inference *n.* (**in**-fer-*uh* ns): a conclusion, assumption or judgment arrived at through a process of reasoning.

📖 The ***inference*** that vaccines cause autism is based on emotion not fact.

momentum *n.* (moh-**men**-t*uh* m): force or speed of movement; strength or progress gained by motion.

📖 Now that 60 people have joined our group, let's schedule some activities before we lose ***momentum***.

outsourcing *v.* (**out**-sohrs-*eng*): to obtain products or services from an outside or external source.

📖 The insurance agent saves time by ***outsourcing*** his social media marketing to attract new business clients.

prerequisite *n.* (*pri*-**rek**-*wuh*-*zit*): a necessary requirement that must be met beforehand.

📖 In the graduation plan for social work, Composition II is a ***prerequisite*** for the professional business writing class.

Vocabulary Exercise #16

Directions: Fill the blank with the correct word.

1. _____ to grow or mature.

2. _____ irritating or harsh.

3. _____ an assumption or conclusion.

4. _____ to highlight or magnify.

5. _____ to give permission.

6. _____ a substitution.

7. _____ a customer.

8. _____ progress gained by motion.

9. _____ a requirement.

10. _____ working with an external source.

Answers: Vocabulary Exercise #16

1. develop

2. strident

3. inference

4. enhance

5. allow

6. replacement

7. consumer

8. momentum

9. prerequisite

10. outsourcing

"Sticks and stones may break our bones,
but words will break our hearts."
-- ROBERT FULGHUM

resignation *n.* (*rez-ig-ney-shuhn*): a formal letter or statement releasing a job, office, title or position; an attitude of submission or non-resistance.

   📖 Bethany emailed her ***resignation*** as minister of music to the pastor.

sufficient *adj.* (s*uh*-**fish**-*uh*nt): adequate enough to meet a need or purpose.

   📖 The teachers received ***sufficient*** copy paper, but not classroom or office supplies.

alternative *n.* (awl-**tur**-n*uh*-tiv): limited choices, usually between two things where only one thing can be chosen.

      alternative *adj.* (awl-**tur**-n*uh*-tiv): different from the usual or conventional; existing or functioning outside of established social or cultural rules.

   📖 Your ***alternative*** to the cafeteria's special of the day is snacks from the vending machine.

contaminate *v.* (k*uh*n-**tam**-*uh*-neyt): to soil, pollute, defile, stain, infect or corrupt; to make something inferior, impure or unfit for use by mixing it with harmful or unclean elements.

   📖Prescription medications ***contaminate*** tap water in most cities.

devise *v.* (dih-**vahyz**): to invent, plot, or form a plan.

   📖 Scammers and liars ***devise*** ways to steal money from innocent people.

environment *n.* (en-**vahy**-r*uh*n-m*uh*nt): outdoor or indoor settings including land, air, people, or other organisms;

the social and cultural conditions that shape and influence individuals and communities.

📕 Global warming is caused by trauma to the earth's ***environment***.

inferior *adj.* (in-**feer**-ee-er): less than; low, poor or substandard quality; lower in rank or position; less important or valuable.

📕 Martha's cubic zirconia wedding ring was ***inferior*** to her sister's diamond, but no one could tell the difference.

monetary *adj.* (**muhn**-i-tair-ee): related to money.

📕 Davenport did not seek ***monetary*** gain for his invention.

overwhelm *v.* (oh-ver-**welm**): to overpower in thought or feeling; to overcome by superior force or numbers; to submerge or bury beneath an excessive amount.

📕 Schools should not ***overwhelm*** children with excessive homework.

presentable *adj.* (pri-**zen**-t*uh*-b*uh*l): fit to be seen; suitable or socially acceptable, especially in appearance.

📕 Put on a tie and blazer to make yourself more ***presentable*** to her parents and church family.

Vocabulary Exercise #17

Directions: Choose the correct definition.

1. resignation

    a) submissive attitude
    b) violence
    c) job interview

2. sufficient

    a) inadequate
    b) overwhelming
    c) enough

3. alternative

    a) a choice
    b) a letter
    c) a decision

4. contaminate

    a) clarify
    b) pollute
    c) poison

5. devise

    a) to meditate
    b) to call
    c) to plot

6. environment

   a) surroundings
   b) cattle
   c) airplanes

7. inferior

   a) high quality
   b) low quality
   c) poor position

8. monetary

   a) related to business
   b) related to money
   c) related to success

9. overwhelm

   a) to bury
   b) to release
   c) to imagine

10. presentable

   a) limited
   b) enormous
   c) acceptable

Answers on the back of this page.

Answers: Vocabulary Exercise #17

1. a

2. c

3. a

4. b

5. c

6. a

7. b

8. b

9. a

10. c

Your Score

_____ correct out of 10

10 – 100%
9 – 90%
8 – 80%
7 – 70%
6 – 60%
5 – 50%
4 – 40%
3 – 30%
2 – 20%
1 – 10%

100%........Excellent
90-80%......Good
70%...........Fair
60%...........Keep Practicing

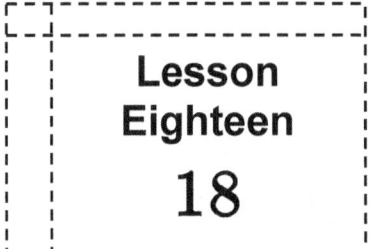

Lesson Eighteen

18

"A synonym is a word you use when you can't spell the word you first thought of."
-- BURT BACHARACH

resource *n.* (*ree-sohrs*): a source of supply or support; information or expertise that can be readily drawn upon when needed; money or assets that can be converted into money.

📖 The guidance counselor is a *resource* for college scholarships.

summarize *v.* (**suhm**-*uh*-rahyz): to shorten and concisely cover the main points; to express in a clear, brief manner.

📖 The manager asked Julian to *summarize* the long grant proposal.

ambivalent *adj.* (am-**biv**-*uh*-luh nt): not able to make a decision; having mixed feelings about someone or something.

📖 Liam and Megan were *ambivalent* about hiring a new editor until they received background checks on all of the candidates for the job.

contemporary *adj.* (kuhn-**tem**-p*uh*-rair-ee): of modern times; about the same age; existing, occurring or living at the same time.

📖 MTV's *contemporary* take on Shakespeare's *Romeo and Juliet* was well received.

diagram *n.* (*dye-uh-gram*): a line drawing that explains mechanical processes and parts.

📖 The *diagram* in the instructions showed how to connect a DVD player to a cable box.

environmental *adj.* (en-**vahy**-r*uh*n-men-tuhl): related to the natural surroundings of the earth or to conditions that influence individuals and communities.

 📖 The declining rain forest presents a huge *environmental* challenge, since 20% of the world's oxygen originates from the Amazon.

informative *adj.* (in-**four**-m*uh*-tiv): full of useful information and knowledge; instructive.

 📖 The *informative* workshop on self-publishing a book was packed.

monumental *adj.* (mon-y*uh*-**men**-tl): having historical or enduring significance; huge or massive; exceptionally great.

 📖 Michael Jackson's *monumental* Motown 25 performance can never be duplicated.

ozone *n.* (**oh**-zohn): a layer of oxygen in the upper atmosphere that absorbs ultraviolet rays and prevents them from reaching the earth's surface.

 📖 Aerosol cans and other environmental pollutants are thinning the *ozone*, which increases global warming.

preserve *v.* (pri-**zurv**): to protect from harm or injury; to keep alive, intact or free from decay; to make something last a long time; to can fruit or food for future use.

  preserve *n.* (pree-**zurv**): canned fruit made into jam or jelly; a restricted area of land that protects natural resources.

 📖 Brides use hairspray to *preserve* their wedding flowers.

Vocabulary Exercise #18

Directions: Match the word from the left column to its correct definition on the right.

1. ____ resources

2. ____ summarize

3. ____ ambivalent

4. ____ contemporary

5. ____ diagram

6. ____ environmental

7. ____ informative

8. ____ monumental

9. ____ ozone

10. ____ preserve

a) instructive

b) hugely significant

c) unable to decide

d) a line drawing

e) to protect

f) of natural surroundings

g) upper atmosphere air

h) of modern times

i) to shorten

j) source of supply

Answers: Vocabulary Exercise #18

1. j

2. i

3. c

4. h

5. d

6. f

7. a

8. b

9. g

10. e

Your Score

_____ correct out of 10

10 – 100%
9 – 90%
8 – 80%
7 – 70%
6 – 60%
5 – 50%
4 – 40%
3 – 30%
2 – 20%
1 – 10%

100%........Excellent
90-80%......Good
70%..........Fair
60%..........Keep Practicing

"All words are pegs to hang ideas on."
-- HENRY WARD BEECHER

restore *v.* (*ri-stohr*): to bring back to a former condition, such as a building, statue, or painting; renew or to bring back to a state of health.

📖 Museum workers want to *restore* old slave records for a new exhibit.

synonym *n.* (**sin**-*uh*-nim): a word that has the same or similar meaning to another word.

📖 The word pollute is a *synonym* for contaminate.

amplify *v.* (**am**-pl*uh*-fye): to make larger, greater, stronger, louder or more visible; to expand by using details or illustrations.

📖 The sound crew had to *amplify* all of the microphones before the concert.

contradictory *adj.* (kon-tr*uh*-**dik**-t*uh*-ree): opposite; inconsistent or does not logically line up.

📖 The police officer's testimony was *contradictory* to the video evidence submitted by the family's defense attorney.

diameter *n.* (*dahy-**am**-i-ter*): the length of a straight, horizontal line that passes through the center of an object, especially a circle.

📖 In geometry, the *diameter* of a circle is two times the radius.

equilibrium *n.* (ee-kw*uh*-**lib**-ree-*uh*m): a state of equal balance; mental or emotional balance.

📖 LaKisha used meditation to find *equilibrium* after her husband died.

inherent *adj.* (in-**hare**-*uh*nt): existing inside someone or something as a natural part of their character or quality.

📖 My child was born with an *inherent* need for independence.

murky *adj.* (**muhr**-kee): characterized by thickness and heaviness of air that makes things difficult to see; dark and gloomy; something that is vague or unclear.

📖 In the early morning, the *murky* woods were filled with animal noises.

provocative *adj.* (pr*uh*-**vok**-*uh*-tiv): serving to excite, stimulate, arouse or to stir up on purpose.

📖 The former aide's *provocative* tell-all book about the white house upset the president's staff.

analyze *v.* (**an**-l-ahyz): to break something down and examine it closely and critically to understand causes, factors, or results.

📖 Literature students *analyze* poems to discover their true meaning.

Vocabulary Exercise #19

Directions: Fill the blank with the correct word.

a) restore   f) equilibrium
b) synonym   g) inherent
c) amplify   h) murky
d) contradictory   i) provocative
e) diameter   j) analyze

1. _____a state of equal balance.

2. _____existing inside something.

3. _____thick, heavy or unclear.

4. _____to carefully examine.

5. _____a word with a same or similar meaning.

6. _____ to bring back to a former condition.

7. _____inconsistent or illogical.

8. _____a line through the center of a circle.

9. _____serving to arouse or stir up.

10. _____to make stronger or louder.

Answers: Vocabulary Exercise #19

1. f—equilibrium

2. g—inherent

3. h—murky

4. j—analyze

5. b—synonym

6. a—restore

7. d—contradictory

8. e—diameter

9. i—provocative

10. c—amplify

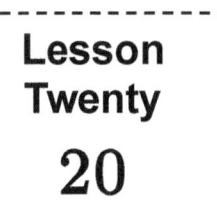

Lesson Twenty

20

annex *v.* (**an**-eks): to make an addition by attaching or joining, especially to something larger or already established.

 📖 The church deacons decided to **annex** the new fellowship hall to the family life center.

convince *v.* (k*uh*n-**vins**): to persuade or change someone's beliefs by using facts, opinion, argument, or emotion.

 📖 It took Maggie three hours to **convince** her parents to loan her their car for the weekend.

differentiate *v.* (dif-*uh*-**ren**-shee-eyt): to identify differences; to mark something in a way that makes it distinct or distinguishes it from others.

 📖 Dr. Taylor painted rainbows on his faculty mailbox to **differentiate** it from the others.

establish *v.* (ih-**stab**-lish): to build on a firm and stable foundation; to settle into a position; to prove something as valid or true.

 📖 Dr. Tracey worked hard to **establish** her medical practice in the suburbs of Atlanta, Georgia instead of her hometown in Arkansas.

inhumanity *n.* (in-hyoo-**man**-i-tee): the state of being cruel to other humans or living beings, lacking warmth and kindness.

 📖 The **inhumanity** of slavery, *The Holocaust* and *The Trail of Tears* reveals the evil that lives in man's heart.

process *n.* (**prah**-sess): a sequence of actions that produce a final result.

📖 The intake *process* at a doctor's office can be long and frustrating.

antonym *n.* (**an**-t*uh*-nim): a word that has the opposite meaning of another word.

📖 Cold is the *antonym* for hot.

coolant *n.* (*koo*-*luh nt*): a liquid used to reduce the temperature of a system by moving heat away from the core, as in an automobile cooling system.

📖 The radiator in Darryl's car overheated, because the *coolant* tank was empty.

dilemma *n.* (dih-**lem**-*uh*): a difficult situation or problem; a choice between two undesirable alternatives.

📖 The *dilemma* to charge poor kids for school lunch can be solved by offering free lunch for everyone through paid community donations.

evident *adj.* (*ev-uh-duhnt*): plain, clear or obvious; easily seen and understood.

📖 The need for gun control is *evident* considering all of the public mass shootings that have occurred this year.

Vocabulary Exercise #20

Directions: Fill the blank with the correct word.

1. _____a difficult situation.

2. _____a sequence of actions.

3. _____to add on.

4. _____plain to see.

5. _____liquid that reduces heat.

6. _____to prove something as true.

7. _____a word with an opposite meaning.

8. _____cruel treatment to living beings.

9. _____to powerfully persuade.

10. _____to make a distinction.

Answers: Vocabulary Exercise #20

1. dilemma

2. process

3. annex

4. evident

5. coolant

6. establish

7. antonym

8. inhumanity

9. convince

10. differentiate

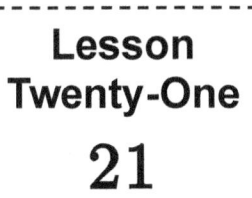

**Lesson
Twenty-One**

21

"A spoken word is not a sparrow.
Once it flies out, you can't catch it."
-- Russian Proverb

evoke *v.* (*ee-vōk*): to summon, call up, or cause to appear, such as memories, feelings or spirits.

 📖 Mahalia Jackson gospel songs *evoke* tears of pain and determination.

innovation *n.* (in-*uh*-**vey**-sh*uh* n): a new creative idea, method, or device that has never been introduced before.

 📖 The technological *innovation* of the iPhone is Steve Jobs' legacy.

protest *n.* (*prōh-test*): an intense expression of disapproval or disagreement in opposition to something a person is powerless to prevent or avoid.

  protest *v.* (*prōh-test*): taking action to show disagreement or disapproval with the intentions to provoke satisfactory changes.

 📖 Colin Kaepernick kneeled during the national anthem at football games to *protest* police brutality and racism against African American men, women, and children.

anxious *adj.* (**angk**-sh*uh*s): worried, showing extreme uneasiness of mind.

 📖 Sierra was so *anxious* about taking the ACT exam for college admissions that she could not eat or sleep for two days prior.

copious *adj.* (**koh**-pee-*uh*s): an abundant supply; plentiful or numerous; a large amount or quantity.

 📖 The boring speaker made *copious* references to the dictionary.

dimension(s) *n.* (dih-**men**-sh*uh*n): measurements in width, length and thickness; scope or importance; a level of existence or consciousness.

📖 The interior designer needs the *dimensions* for the replacement rug.

excellent *adj.* (**ek**-s*uh*-lu*h*nt): superior or first-class; possessing outstanding quality; extremely good.

📖 The chef's vegan stir fry was *excellent* and satisfied the customers.

insignificant *adj.* (in-sig-**nif**-i-k*uh*nt): too small to be important; petty; without the weight of importance.

📖 *Insignificant* comments on Trisha's cooking videos did not stop her from securing a major brand deal.

appeal *n.* (*uh*-**peel**): an earnest request for help, support, sympathy or mercy.

    appeal *v.* (*uh*-**peel**): to have a lower court's decision reviewed in a higher court.

📖 Steve's *appeal* for detention instead of suspension fell on deaf ears.

corporate *adj.* (**kohr**-per-it): united or combined into one; related to a business association of employers and employees that belong to a particular industry.

📖 Three churches held a *corporate* prayer rally for child safety and school improvement in their community.

Vocabulary Exercise #21

Directions: Circle **correct** or **incorrect** for each definition below. Write the appropriate definition, if incorrect.

1. **excellent:** superior quality.

   a) correct
   b) incorrect

2. **anxious:** calm and peaceful.

   a) correct
   b) incorrect

3. **corporate:** related to a business.

   a) correct
   b) incorrect

4. **protest:** a demonstration of agreement.

   a) correct
   b) incorrect

5. **appeal:** an earnest request.

   a) correct
   b) incorrect

6. **innovation:** a creative idea.

    a) correct
    b) incorrect

7. **dimension:** a level of existence.

    a) correct
    b) incorrect

8. **insignificant:** of great importance.

    a) correct
    b) incorrect

9. **copious:** insufficient or scarce supply.

    a) correct
    b) incorrect

10. **evoke:** to bring something forth.

    a) correct
    b) incorrect

Answers on the back of this page.

Sign up for **"Student Success Writing Skills"** at www.arhampton.com/classes.

Answers: Vocabulary Exercise #21

1. a—correct

2. b—incorrect

3. a—correct

4. b—incorrect

5. a—correct

6. a—correct

7. a—correct

8. b—incorrect

9. b—incorrect

10. a—correct

Your Score

_____ correct out of 10

10 – 100%
9 – 90%
8 – 80%
7 – 70%
6 – 60%
5 – 50%
4 – 40%
3 – 30%
2 – 20%
1 – 10%

100%........Excellent
90-80%......Good
70%...........Fair
60%...........Keep Practicing

"There's nothing to writing. All you do is sit down at a typewriter and open a vein." – RED SMITH

counseling *n.* (*koun-suh-ling*): professional guidance in resolving personal conflicts and emotional problems.

📖 Family **counseling** after her parents' divorce allowed Meredith to focus better in school.

diminish *v.* (dih-**min**-ish): to decrease or make less; to lessen the authority, dignity or reputation of someone or something.

📖 Even ten years after his death, people try to **diminish** the awesome accomplishments of the King of Pop, Michael Jackson.

except *prep.* (ek-**sept**): to be left out; with the exclusion of someone or something.

📖 Bring all of the fruit to the kitchen table **except** the rotten ones.

instill *v.* (in-**steel**): to gradually fill or infuse into the mind or feelings; to cause to enter drop by drop.

📖 Try volunteering at animal shelters to **instill** kindness in your children.

apply *v.* (*uh-plahy*): to put to use for a particular purpose; to have relevance or a valid connection; to make a request in the form of a written application.

📖 Theo needs to **apply** animated graphic design skills to his next project before he can **apply** for the creative director position.

countenance *n.* (**koun**-tuh-n*uh*ns): the appearance of a person's face, especially facial expressions.

 📖 The model's *countenance* in the photo was calm and serene.

disgust *v.* (dis-**guhst**): to cause extreme dislike, loathing or nausea; to offend good taste or morals.

 📖 Comedy shows with too much cursing and foul language *disgust* me.

exploits *n.* (**eks**-ploit): notable or heroic acts.

 📖 The *exploits* of the slave Sojourner Truth within the underground railroad are worth teaching and remembering.

internal *adj.* (*in-**tur**-nl*): existing inside or in the inner parts; inside of the body.

 📖 The *internal* fighting between the owners and managers caused the family-owned drugstore chain to close.

apprehensive *adj.* (ap-ri-**hen**-siv): uneasy or fearful about something that might happen.

 📖 Since Tiffany was *apprehensive* about going to the party, she decided to stay at home.

Vocabulary Exercise #22

Directions: Match the word from the left column to its correct definition on the right.

1. ____ apprehensive

2. ____ internal

3. ____ exploits

4. ____ disgust

5. ____ countenance

6. ____ apply

7. ____ instill

8. ____ except

9. ____ diminish

10. ____ counseling

a) to infuse in the mind

b) facial expressions

c) to cause dislike

d) uneasy or fearful

e) professional guidance

f) heroic acts

g) to lessen

h) with the exclusion of

i) to put to use

j) on the inside

Answers: Vocabulary Exercise #22

1. d

2. j

3. f

4. c

5. b

6. i

7. a

8. h

9. g

10. e

Your Score

_____ correct out of 10

10 – 100%
9 – 90%
8 – 80%
7 – 70%
6 – 60%
5 – 50%
4 – 40%
3 – 30%
2 – 20%
1 – 10%

100%........Excellent
90-80%......Good
70%...........Fair
60%...........Keep Practicing

"Words, like eyeglasses, blur everything that they don't make more clear."
-- Joseph Joubert

apprise *v.* (*uh*-**pryze**): to inform, tell, make aware, or give notice.

 📖 Before you leave, please *apprise* human resources of your travel plans and return date.

create *v.* (kree-**eight**): to make or bring something new into existence; to produce from skill and imagination; to provoke or cause something to happen.

 📖 *Create* bold art that will *create* lasting changes in your community.

dispose *v.* (dih-**spōhz**): to get rid of; to give a tendency to or incline toward, such as illness or temperament.

 📖 Germs in the air *dispose* newborn babies to sickness and disease.

external *adj.* (ek-**stur**-nl): on the outside or the outer part; outside of the body.

 📖 This eye cream is for *external* use only.

arrange *v.* (*uh*-**reynj**): to place in proper order; to prepare or plan; to come to an agreement or understanding.

 📖 Juda will *arrange* for the airfare while I *arrange* his clothes in the suitcase.

credit *n.* (**kred**-it): an amount added to an account; the provision of money, goods or services with the expectation of future payment; special recognition.

credit *v.* (**kred**-it): to recognize or acknowledge; to consider as the source; to add to an account.

📖 Peter and Marissa *credit* the school secretary for the $50 *credit* on their child's lunch account.

disproportionate *adj.* (dis-pr*uh*-**pōre**-sh*uh*-nit): unequal or out of balance; lacking symmetry.

📖 J.A. Fair High School expels a *disproportionate* number of black male students every year.

extinction *n.* (ik-**stingk**-sh*uh* n): the condition of being out of existence; the process of dying out or coming to an end.

📖 Melting snow and warm temperatures in the Artic Circle could mean the *extinction* of polar bears.

investigate *v.* (in-**ves**-ti-geyt): to examine or study in detail; to search out the facts in attempts to find an explanation.

📖 The police will *investigate* the robbery to find a suspect.

articulate *adj.* (ahr-**tik**-y*uh*-lit): clear and distinct, especially when speaking and pronouncing words.

articulate *v.* (ahr-**tik**-y*uh*-leyt): to speak clearly and effectively; to put into words.

📖 The *articulate* pastor's sermon helped Bill to *articulate* his problems with organized religion.

Vocabulary Exercise #23

Directions: Write the word for each definition in the space provided.

1. to produce something new

2. dying out

3. to inform or make aware

4. to get rid of

5. to search or examine

6. clear or distinct

7. on the outside

8. out of balance

9. to give recognition

10. to place properly

Answers: Vocabulary Exercise #23

1. create

2. extinction

3. apprise

4. dispose

5. investigate

6. articulate

7. external

8. disproportionate

9. credit

10. arrange

"Words are as beautiful as wild horses,
and sometimes as difficult to corral."
-- TED BERKMAN

assessment *n.* (*uh*-**ses**-m*uh* nt): an appraisal, evaluation or test; a valuation of property for tax purposes.

📖 The teacher created a writing skills ***assessment*** to see how much students knew about grammar.

crevice *n.* (**krev**-is): a narrow opening caused by a crack or a split.

📖 Two roaches slid into a ***crevice*** in the kitchen cabinet.

dissect *v.* (dye-**sekt**): to cut open to examine the parts, such as a human or animal body; to closely analyze.

📖 Jeremy flunked biology, because he could not ***dissect*** a dead frog.

assume *v.* (*uh*-**soom**): to believe something without proof; to take over responsibility; to place yourself in (a position).

📖 You need to ***assume*** the insurance payments for your car.

critical *adj.* (**krit**-i-k*uh*l): judgmental; tending to find fault or to judge harshly; approaching a crisis or death.

📖 Tina's daughter is in ***critical*** condition after her premature birth.

distinction *n.* (dih-**stingk**-*shuhn*): a special honor, recognition, award, or accomplishment; differences or the condition of being different from others; the recognizing or noticing of differences.

📖 The ***distinction*** of being a *Donaghey Scholars* graduate distinguished her from other law school applicants.

atmosphere *n.* (**at**-m*uh*s-feer): the whole mass of air surrounding the earth; a surrounding influence in an environment.

📖 Reggae music creates an ***atmosphere*** of joy and celebration.

cultured *adj.* (**kuhl**-cherd): upscale, refined and well-rounded; having an intellectual knowledge of arts, classical music, the humanities, and the finer things in life.

📖 The rapper Snoop Dogg is actually more ***cultured*** and well-read than he appears.

domestic *adj.* (d*uh*-**mes**-tik): related or devoted to the home, family or household affairs; not wild, but tame.

    domestic *n.* (d*uh*-**mes**-tik): a hired household servant; something produced in one's own country.

📖 Linda's love for gardening and ***domestic*** projects prompted her to hire a Nigerian ***domestic*** who favored ***domestic*** white wine.

involve *v.* (in-**volv**): to include as necessary; to engage as a participant.

📖 LaVeda does not ***involve*** herself in Cedrick's business affairs.

Vocabulary Exercise #24

Directions: Choose the correct meaning.

1. assessment

   a) a test
   b) a report
   c) a book

2. crevice

   a) a pit
   b) a crack
   c) a crater

3. dissect

   a) to kneel
   b) to fill
   c) to cut

4. assume

   a) to trust
   b) to believe
   c) to criticize

5. critical

   a) judgmental
   b) tolerant
   c) biased

6. distinction

    a) a credit

    b) an award

    c) a deduction

7. atmosphere

    a) the galaxy

    b) the earth

    c) the air

8. cultured

    a) refined

    b) rough

    c) smooth

9. domestic

    a) wild

    b) tame

    c) quiet

10. involve

    a) to include

    b) to exclude

    c) to appeal

Answers on the back of this page.

Answers: Vocabulary Exercise #24

1. a

2. b

3. c

4. b

5. a

6. b

7. c

8. a

9. b

10. a

Your Score

_____ correct out of 10

10 – 100%
9 – 90%
8 – 80%
7 – 70%
6 – 60%
5 – 50%
4 – 40%
3 – 30%
2 – 20%
1 – 10%

100%........Excellent
90-80%......Good
70%..........Fair
60%..........Keep Practicing

Lesson Twenty-Five

25

"If you believe in the power of words, you can bring about physical changes in the universe." – N. Scott Momaday

attrition *n.* (*uh*-**trish**-*uh* n): a reduction in numbers, usually from retirement, resignation or death; sorrow for sins or bad behavior.

> 📖 We need to hire younger professors to fight *attrition* in the English department.

currency *n.* (**kuhr**-*uh* n-see): money or something that is circulated as a form of exchange.

> 📖 Creative expression is the *currency* among artists, not money.

augment *v.* (awg-**ment**): to increase or enlarge in size, number, strength or length.

> 📖 Dabnis offered to work overtime to *augment* his salary.

current *adj.* (**kuhr**-*uh*nt): most recent; existing or happening at the present time.

> 📖 Buy the *current* issue of *Essence Magazine* for the waiting room.

aural *adj.* (*awr-uhl*): relating to the ear or sense of hearing.

> 📖 Listening to smooth jazz music on Sunday is an *aural* pleasure.

cynicism *n.* (**sin**-*uh*-siz-*uh* m): a bitter attitude; distrust of people and their motives, especially ones that seem positive.

> 📖 Pamela's wedding announcement to her co-workers was met with *cynicism* and snide remarks.

donate *v.* (**dōh**-neyt): to give or contribute (to a cause or charity).

📖 Our sorority will *donate* $1,000 per month to the local food bank.

awareness *n.* (*uh-**wair**-nis*): a conscious, alert knowledge about what is happening.

📖 Activists use social media to raise *awareness* of racial discrimination.

dupe *n.* (doop): a person who is easily deceived or cheated.

    dupe *v.* (doop): to trick, cheat or defraud.

📖 The sales guy thought I was a *dupe*, and tried to *dupe* me into buying a used car with bad brakes.

attractive *adj.* (*uh-**trak**-tiv*): having a pleasing appearance and the ability to draw toward; charming or magnetic.

📖 The comedian's *attractive* personality impresses talent agents.

Vocabulary Exercise #25

Directions: Fill the blank with the correct word.

1. _____to increase.

2. _____to give or contribute.

3. _____the most recent.

4. _____charming or magnetic.

5. _____a conscious knowledge.

6. _____of the ear.

7. _____a reduction in numbers.

8. _____money or a form of exchange.

9. _____a bitter distrust of people.

10. _____to trick or deceive.

Answers: Vocabulary Exercise #25

1. augment

2. donate

3. current

4. attractive

5. awareness

6. aural

7. attrition

8. currency

9. cynicism

10. dupe

Your Score

_____ correct out of 10

10 – 100%
9 – 90%
8 – 80%
7 – 70%
6 – 60%
5 – 50&
4 – 40%
3 – 30%
2 – 20%
1 – 10%

100%........Excellent
90-80%......Good
70%...........Fair
60%...........Keep Practicing

More Resources from
Ashan R. Hampton

B & W Print
ISBN: 978-0-359-69282-8

Have you been out of the classroom for a while? *Adult Learner Grammar Essentials* teaches you to effectively correct the most common grammar errors encountered in academic writing.

With self-study quizzes, plain English explanations and real-world examples, you will improve your grammar skills in just minutes a day.

Ordering information:

www.arhampton.com/books
www.lulu.com

B & W Print
ISBN: 978-1-387-95472-8

Can you catch mistakes in your own writing? Do you know how to identify and correct common writing errors? Would you like to become an effective proofreader for personal growth or profit?

Proofreading Power: Skills & Drills provides essential rules, guidelines and tips to quickly boost your editing prowess.

Ordering information:

www.arhampton.com/books
www.lulu.com

References

Hampton, Ashan R. *Grammar Essentials for Proofreading, Copyediting & Business Writing*. Little Rock: Cornerstone Communications & Publishing, 2018. Print.

Merriam-Webster's Collegiate Dictionary, 11th edition. Springfield, Massachusetts: Merriam-Webster, Inc., 2014. Print.

Index

www.ingramcontent.com/pod-product-compliance
Lightning Source LLC
Chambersburg PA
CBHW080415290526
45791CB00008BA/2282